deleted

War of 1812

Edited by
Mary Alice Burke Robinson

American troops, fighting the British at the Battle of Chippewa.

Discovery Enterprises, Ltd.
Carlisle, Massachusetts

© Discovery Enterprises, Ltd., Carlisle, MA 1998

ISBN 1-57960-007-7 paperback edition
Library of Congress Catalog Card Number 97-77858

10   9   8   7   6   5   4   3   2   1

Printed in the United States of America

Subject Reference Guide:

War of 1812
edited by Mary Alice Burke Robinson

War of 1812 — U.S. History

Native Americans — U.S. History

Photo/Illustration Credits:

Cover art - The Battle of Tippecanoe strengthened Native American resistance.

All illustrations and photo credits are from the National Archives,
except as otherwise cited where they appear in the text.

Dedication:

To My Family

Table of Contents

Why War?

by
Mary Alice Burke Robinson

Shortly after the end of the American Revolution, Britain became caught up in another war on the continent of Europe: the Napoleonic Wars. The young United States entered into a period of economic growth and prosperity. But before long, the struggle between Britain and France began to have repercussions in America.

Britain did not want war with the United States but neither did she want to back down on her policies of curtailing trade or impressment of American sailors. Besides boarding American ships and confiscating cargoes, the British were capturing and virtually enslaving American seamen on the grounds that they were British deserters or British citizens. Sometimes these charges were true, but many times the action was simply a way of rounding out crews on British ships, to strengthen their forces against France. Naturally, impressment was resented by the United States.

Britain, even while fighting Napoleon, was still very much in a position of power. She had the world's strongest navy and well-trained, capable officers. She had control of the Great Lakes; a regular army in the Maritime Provinces of 4,300; 5,600 regulars in Upper and Lower Canada; and the support of most western Indian tribes. Sir George Prevost, governor of Upper and Lower Canada, thought he could rely on 400 out of the 11,000 in his militia, and knew that he had more support in Lower Canada (Quebec) than in Upper Canada (Ontario), where so much of the population was actually American.

Britain was aware of the source of Upper Canada's growth, and was also unsure of her loyalty. Most people living in Upper Canada were of American heritage, having arrived after the American Revolution, not for political reasons, but for the opportunity to purchase cheap land. Therefore, Britain did not dare call up local militia for fear that they might refuse to fight against Americans. Major General Isaac Brock, commander of the forces and chief administrator in Upper Canada, was reluctant to actually arm more than 4,000 of the 11,000 men in his militia units.

Typical of this time, many Canadians were hesitant about taking a stand against their neighbors from the south. P. Finan's father was an officer at York when it was attacked by Americans. Along with others, the twelve-year-old Finan left York for Kingston, Ontario, after the burning and looting of York. On their journey, they found few Canadians who were sympathetic to the British refugees. Years later, Finan wrote a journal in which he recalled his experience of traveling through Ontario.

Source: John Gellner, editor, *Recollections of The War of 1812: Three Eyewitnesses' Accounts,* Toronto: Baxter, 1964, originally published between 1828 and 1854, p. 98.

The majority of the inhabitants of this part of the country evinced great disloyalty as we proceeded, being much gratified with the success of the Americans; and, considering they had nothing to fear from us, did not hesitate to avow it. In many instances they concealed their horses, waggons, &c. in the woods, to avoid accommodating us with them, and told us they had none. ...my father, who was very much exasperated....On threatening the proprietor to have him deprived of his property and expelled from the country, he very deliberately brought a couple of waggons, well appointed, out of the wood, after protesting, a short time before, that he had no such thing.

In spite of the fact that New England states were the most affected by curtailment of shipping and impressment of her sailors, residents of the north-eastern United States were against going to war. If America sided with the French under the despot Napoleon, she would appear to turn her back on all the democratic principles which had so recently been defended in the American Revolution.

Many from the South and West, however, looked hungrily at Spanish-held Florida, which at that time extended to the Mississippi River. Florida would make a great addition to the Union, and after all, Spain allied itself with Britain in the European war. So many from the West and South, with an eye on U. S. expansion, were eager to fight against Britain.

Northeasterners realized that U. S. trade was booming with Canada and Britain, using the St. Lawrence River as a comparatively easy route to Montreal. Sailors and merchants on the coast saw war as a potential economic disaster, as did Americans along the Great Lakes and St. Lawrence River.

For much of the U. S.- Canadian border, there was no way of knowing exactly where the border was along northern New York, Vermont, New Hampshire, or Maine. People passed freely back and forth, even when they did recognize the boundary (as along the Great Lakes and the St. Lawrence River). So, for local merchants, even during the war, it was "business as usual."

The United States had a weak army and navy, poor officers, poorly-trained and half-hearted militia, and lack of strong leadership from the President James Madison. Fewer than 7,000 men were in army units. Four hundred thousand were listed as being in state militias, but that figure was totally unreliable. The navy had 20 vessels and some gunboats. Congress voted to increase the army to 35,000 but neglected to provide the money to recruit and equip them. Later Congress promised a $40 bounty and 160 acres of land (three months' pay in advance) but still there was little enthusiasm about joining. By the end of 1812, there were only 15,000 soldiers.

James Madison

President Madison wanted to take Montreal, to bottle up access to the Great Lakes and the West. One major reason that President Madison's plan was not used was that such an attack on Montreal involved taking troops and supplies through New York and New England, where opposition to the war was so strong that there was the possibility of open hostility from Americans there. The governors of Massachusetts and Connecticut refused to send militia to take part in any offensive military action. Most New England militia were not called during the war as it was very uncertain that their help would be forthcoming.

Border Trade Continued

All during the war, trade with Canada was brisk. Northern New Yorkers could get their produce to Montreal via the St. Lawrence River much more easily than getting it to New York City. After the war began, and throughout its duration, farmers of New York and Vermont supplied the British army with their goods.

A British army officer stationed at Prescott (Fort Wellington) in January 1814 wrote of the trade across the St. Lawrence River.

> The country is so excessively poor that our supplies are all drawn from the American side of the river....They drive droves of cattle from the interior under pretence of supplying the (U. S.) army at Salmon River and are so allowed to pass the guards, and at night to pass them over to our side.

Ogdensburg, New York lies across a narrow part of the St. Lawrence River, within sight of Prescott, Ontario. Canadians could easily skate or walk across to Ogdensburg in winter, or row a boat across in summer. Visiting friends and relatives on the other side of the river was a pleasant afternoon's excursion. Canadians shopped at David Parish's store in Ogdensburg.

Ogdensburg was raided by troops, civilians, and Indians on February 22, 1813 in retaliation for some earlier raids by soldiers from the little garrison at Ogdensburg. David Parish was indignant at the inconvenience of the raids and, in a letter to his Ogdensburg agent, Joseph Rosseel, he blamed them on the indiscretion of the commanding officer.

Source: *David Parish Papers*, Fort Wellington, Prescott, Ontario.

> I trust that men of more discretion and prudence will in future be selected to command on Our frontiers — I have represented this Subject in strong Language to several members of the Cabinet & trust that it will be duly attended to.

After the raid, the good citizens of Ogdensburg asked their government to remove American troops from their town because stationing them in Ogdensburg caused too much trouble between the citizens in that town and their friends, relatives and neighbors across the river at Prescott. The government did bow to the request. From then on, the British military and navy could freely travel up and down the St. Lawrence near Prescott. That was agreeable to Joseph Rosseel, as business was booming!

Source: *Ibid.*, 27 March, 1813, 23 July, 1814.

The frequent communications if continued will do good to our villagers. The officers for instance are getting new Boots made & old ones mended here...

....

It is incredible what quantities of Cattle & Sheep are driven into Canada we can hardly get any thing for love or money. The day before yesterday upwards of 100 Oxen went up through Prescott and yesterday above 200.

It is significant that American merchants knew that war had been declared before American officers were informed. Agents and business partners had sent word, which travelled faster than those sent by official routes.

Because of the lack of interest, or outright antipathy toward war in the North and Northeast, American leaders decided to concentrate on the West, where there was enthusiasm for the war and where the Canadians had a weaker presence.

Note from the publisher: Due to space restrictions, this book concentrates on the land wars fought during the War of 1812, however, the naval battles are worth looking at more closely, as well. Check the sources suggested at the back of this book for other materials which will contribute to your further study of this war.

The documents excerpted here are intact as far as their original spelling and grammar are concerned. A line of dots indicates the omission of at least one paragraph.

War Hawks

That the United States did go to war at all is largely due to a group of young Congressmen known as the War Hawks, who were eager for further expansion of the U. S. They represented people who wanted to extend settlement but were worried about the Indians on the frontier. And, they had reason to be worried. There had been vicious raids on white settlements, and retaliation on their part which showed signs of such escalation that no one was safe. On the frontier both settlers and Indians lived in constant fear of attack.

The War Hawks thought that an invasion of Canada would be easy and result in its annexation. The United States had six million people, not counting slaves, while in all of Canada there were only 500,000. The War Hawks were counting on Canadians to want, or at least not object to, annexation. And they gambled that Britain's best officers and soldiers would be on the battlefields of Europe rather than at tiny outposts in Canada.

Britain wanted to contain the young United States within boundaries established at the end of the American Revolution. Her government proposed creating an independent state for American Indians along the U. S.-Canadian border, which would serve as a buffer zone and a deterrent to any American attempt to invade and overpower Canada. For this reason, most Indian tribes sided with Britain.

Some Indians recognized that if they did not resist, they would lose all their land. They also realized that their own inter-tribal warfare had to be set aside while they faced a common enemy. Two leaders of this movement were the Shawnee, Tenskwatawa, called The Prophet, and his elder brother, Tecumseh. They worked to form an Indian federation that would be powerful enough to halt white encroachment on Indian lands.

Tecumseh explained his philosophy in a speech addressed to William Henry Harrison in August of 1810.

Tecumseh's Speech
to William Henry Harrison, 1810

Source: Tecumseh, August 12, 1810, in Samuel G. Drake, *Biography and History of the Indians of North America*, 11th ed., Boston, 1841, pp. 617-618.

I would say to him [Gov. Harrison], Sir, you have liberty to return to your own country. The being within, communing with past ages, tells me, that once, nor until lately, there was no white man on this continent. That it then all belonged to red men, children of the same parents, placed on it by the Great Spirit that made them, to keep it, to traverse it, to enjoy its productions, and to fill it with the same race. Once a happy race. Since made miserable by the white people, who are never contented, but always encroaching. The way, and the only way to check and stop this evil, is, for all the red men to unite in claiming a common and equal right in the land, as it was at first, and should be yet; for it never was divided, but belongs to all, for the use of each. That no part has a right to sell, even to each other, much less to strangers; those who want all, and will not do with less.

The white people have no right to take the land from the Indians, because they had it first; it is theirs. They may sell, but all must join. Any sale not made by all is not valid. The late sale is bad. It was made by a part only. Part do not know how to sell. It requires all to make a bargain for all. All red men have equal rights to the unoccupied land. The right of occupancy is as good in one place as in another. There cannot be two occupations in the same place. The first excludes all others. It is not so in hunting or travelling; for there the same ground will serve many, as they may follow each other all day; but the camp is stationary, and that is occupancy. It belongs to the first who sits down on his blanket or skins, which he has thrown upon the ground, and till he leaves it no other has a right.

Pushmataha, a Choctaw Chief, Opposes War with the United States (1811)

Pushmataha
(Courtesy of the National Archives)

Some Indian tribes felt that Tecumseh should not encourage Indians to join with the British in their struggles against the United States. When Tecumseh went south in 1811 to gain Indian support against the Americans in the Northeast, Choctaw Chief Pushmataha opposed Tecumseh's plan. He urged his tribesmen to look beyond past injustices, refuse to commit themselves to joining with the British, and look ahead to a peaceful future with the White man.

Source: H. B. Cushman, *History of the Choctaw, Chickasaw, and Natchez Indians*, Greenville, Texas, 1899, pp. 315-318. Found in Steven Mintz, ed., *Native American Voices*, St. James, New York: Brandywine Press, 1995. pp. 99-100.

The question before us now is not what wrongs they have inflicted upon our race, but what measures are best for us to adopt in regard to them; and though our race may have been unjustly treated and shamefully wronged by them [the whites], yet I shall not for that reason alone advise you to destroy them unless it was just and wise for you so to do; nor would I advise you to forgive them, though worthy of your commiseration, unless I believe it would be to the interest of our common good....

My friends and fellow countrymen! you now have no just cause to declare war against the American people, or wreak your vengeance upon them as enemies, since they have ever manifested feelings of friendship towards you. It is...a disgrace to the memory of your forefathers, to wage war against the American people merely to gratify the malice of the English.

The war, which you are now contemplating against the Americans...forebodes nothing but destruction to our entire race. It is a war against a people whose territories are now far greater than our own, and who are far better provided with all the necessary implements of war, with men, guns, horses, wealth, far beyond that of all our race combined, and where is the necessity or wisdom to make war upon such a people?

Tippecanoe

While Tecumseh was in the South trying to gather Creek, Choctaw, and Cherokee support, General William Henry Harrison, the governor of the Indiana Territory, led an attack on The Prophet's village on Tippecanoe Creek, in December 1811. In a letter to the governor of Kentucky, Harrison told of his reason for going there, of the surprise night attack, and of the bloodbath that followed. With chilling objectivity he stated the main intent of the expedition.

Source: *America; Great Crises in Our History Told By Its Makers*, Vol. V, Americanization Department, Veterans of Foreign Wars of the United States, Chicago, 1925, pp. 106-112.

It has been said that the Indians should have been attacked upon our arrival before their town, on the evening of the 6th. There were two reasons which prevented this, first, that the directions which I received from the government, made it necessary that I should endeavor, if possible, to accomplish the object of the expedition (the dispersion of the Prophet's force) without bloodshed, and secondly, that the success of an attack by day upon the town was problematical....

5000-6000 Indians made a surprise night attack....I did believe that they would not attack us that night....I expected that they would have met me the next day to hear my terms, but I did not believe, however, that they would accede to them — and it was my determination to attack and burn the town the following night. It was necessary therefore that the troops would be refreshed as much as possible.

Thus Harrison, in his own words, stated that his orders were to disperse the Indians without bloodshed, but his plan was to make demands that were so extreme that the Indians would not accept them. That would give Harrison the excuse to destroy the village, and scatter The Prophet's braves. The government's orders were probably impossible to carry out; still, Harrison's plan went far beyond official government orders.

Two hundred white men were killed and wounded in that attack. The number of Indian casualties was never known. Although the defeat served to reinforce Indian unity in the struggle against the Americans, this was a victory for General Harrison, who was hailed a hero. During his campaign for the office of President of the United States, the slogan, "Tippecanoe and Tyler too" was a reminder that William Henry Harrison was a military hero and a man who "got things done!"

In this campaign he was supported by another military hero and Indian fighter who would also become president, General Andrew Jackson. Jackson had defeated the Creeks in a battle on the Wabash which established his fame. His leadership and victory at the final conflict in the War of 1812, the Battle of New Orleans, gave him an even more prominent place in America's history.

The Dearborn Massacre

In November 1811, at Tippecanoe Creek, William Henry Harrison attacked a stronghold of The Prophet, Tecumseh's brother, laying waste to the buildings and winter stores. It was too late in the season for the Indians to strike back, but there was no doubt that retaliation would come in Spring.

On June 18, 1812, war was declared by the United States on Britain.

General Hull surrendered Detroit on August 16, 1812, but had earlier sent orders to Captain Nathan Heald, the commandant of Fort Dearborn, to abandon the fort and take everyone there to Detroit. Dearborn was too isolated to get help if attacked.

Orders to evacuate tiny Fort Dearborn (where Michigan Avenue and River Street in present day Chicago meet) were received by Captain Heald on August 7, 1812, yet he did not order an evacuation until the 14th, a delay which gave the Indians time to gather. Captain Heald agreed to leave all provisions for the Indians, except those needed by his men on the evacuation route. In return, the Indians agreed to provide a safe escort. But Heald was in for a big surprise.

"Linden Birds Have Been Singing"

August 15, 1812

The family of a young officer was among the small group of people preparing to leave Fort Dearborn. Years later, Susan Simmons, a baby at the time of the evacuation, set down the recollections of her mother.

Source: M. D. Simmons, *Heroes and Heroines of the Fort Dearborn Massacre*, Journal Publishing Company, 1896, pp. 29, 33, 34, 37, 46-59.

Black Partridge, a Pottawatamie chief, warned Capt. Heald that the young braves were eager to attack. He said that "...young men had determined to wash their hands in the blood of the whites...," and that he could not restrain them. Then he closed his remarkable speech with the most emphatic warning, saying: "Linden birds have been singing in my ears to-day; be careful on the march you are about to make." The fact that near five hundred armed warriors had collected in the immediate vicinity of the fort itself boded no good to the garrison, but the warning of Black Partridge, couched in the most significant language and delivered in terms of sadness ...should have changed doubt...in the mind of Captain Heald into positive certainty.

The group that left the fort that fateful morning consisted of 54 regular soldiers, 12 militia, and a small number of civilians, including 18 children. With them was Captain William Wells who had gathered a few Miami braves and hurried to Fort Dearborn. His niece was the wife of Capt. Heald. He arrived too late to convince the commander to change his plans, but agreed to travel with them as added protection.

Capt. Wells discovered about a mile and a half away from the fort that Indians were preparing to attack from behind a line of sand hills as the little band travelled along the bank of Lake Michigan. After a short battle, they surrendered to 684 Indians who, that very morning, had accepted the rations given them by the army, and had promised safe passage.

When the attack began:

...the baggage train, with the women and children remained near the lake, with the twelve militia men and a mere handful of regulars to guard them....The savages soon discovered the almost defenseless condition of the baggage train and of the women and children, fired a volley upon them and then rushed in from front, rear and right, with uplifted tomahawks. The few soldiers having discharged their rifles and being too closely pressed to reload them, continued the unequal contest with clubbed guns until every one was slain.

It was at this time that the brave Capt. Wells returned through the Indian lines to the defense of the women and children, and dealt death among the savages until covered with wounds he fell with his face to the enemy, confronting death as a brave knight in defense of the helpless....His Miami Indians had betrayed him and fled to the enemy, leaving him to battle and die alone.

At the first fire from the Indians Mrs. Holt was wounded in the foot and was rendered unable to walk when the charge was made upon the guard protecting the women and children. The savages came on enmasse firing their guns and uttering hideous yells. The horses harnessed to the wagons became ungovernable and ran over Mrs. Holt, trampling her to death. Mrs. Bell was also severely and perhaps fatally wounded and finally tomahawked to death. Her husband, a soldier, was slain in action, leaving little Peter Bell, a boy six years old, the lone survivor of the family,...The boy was fortunately on foot and thus escaped the doom which fell upon all within the wagon. Three children besides those in the wagon were murdered on the spot, leaving six prisoners. Of these but two drifted back to civilization, Peter Bell and the infant babe of Mrs. Simmons, which escaped the fate of her little brother and the other children by being held in the arms of her mother during the massacre....

The Indians now proceeded to deliberately hack and mangle to death five of the captured and disarmed soldiers...Mrs. Simmons discovered that the delight of the savages was much enhanced by tormenting their prisoners in every conceivable manner,....She therefore summoned all her marvelous fortitude to prevent any expression of the anguish which was crushing her great soul...during the entire period of her captivity, eight long months, she met all the insults and injuries of her captors with defiance, never once during that period paying them the tribute of a tear.

The dead were stripped of everything of value, were scalped and their scalps were strung on a pole and carried on their march as trophies of the campaign. The march was then made back to the fort, where the Indians camped for the night, and feasted on the stores, while around and near the old Massacre Tree lay stark in death thirty-eight soldiers, twelve children and two women,....

In the morning the plunder was divided and the prisoners were separated, some going to the Kankakee village, some to Green Bay, and some to Michigan. After moving out of the fort it was set on fire and burned, and the line of march for the respective villages was taken up. It fell to the lot of Mrs. Simmons to go to Green

Bay...the hardships of the journey to Mrs. Simmons consisted mainly in being compelled to do the drudgery of the Indians, such as gathering fuel, building fires and preparing food. On the march she walked and carried her babe, the entire distance being over two hundred miles.

They finally reached the village...soon, old and young, male and female, were on the open ground outside the circle of wigwams and formed a long double line reaching to the verge of the surrounding pines. The prisoners were then marched to one end of the line and each one of the soldiers was compelled to run the gauntlet receiving blows from the women and children who formed the line, and who beat them with sticks, switches and clubs. Mrs. Simmons witnessed this...to her dismay she was led...to the starting point....It was an awful moment for the poor woman, but...as if inspired with superhuman strength, she wrapped the blanket about the babe...and folding it in her strong arms to protect it,...she ran rapidly down the line, reaching the goal bleeding and bruised, but with the beloved object of her solicitude unharmed.

Immediately after passing the gauntlet Mrs. Simmons was astonished to receive an act of kindness for the first time since her captivity began. An elderly squaw took her kindly by the arm and led her into a wigwam, where her wounds and bruises were washed, food was given her and she was permitted to lie down and enjoy as well as she could a much needed rest....Mrs. Simmons ever after spoke of her as the Indian mother....

...she was sent in midwinter from Mackinac to Detroit, a distance of over three hundred miles....Her clothing was woefully insufficient and in tatters, the weather was unendurable, and food so scarce that she often appeased hunger by eating roots, acorns and nuts found under the snow. Her babe, now a year old, had much increased in weight, yet with her own diminished strength she was obliged to carry it in her arms continually while she performed the camp drudgery for the Indians.

Late in March she arrived at Fort Meigs....Here Mrs. Simmons ...joyfully learned that a supply train had just arrived from Cincinnati, and would immediately return under a strong escort. The train was to pass on return within a few miles of her home in Miami county, Ohio.

On a day about the middle of April, 1813, the train passed four miles south of her home. Here she left the wagons...and taking her babe in her arms walked swiftly along a dim path through the forest. ...As her heart burned within her at the remembrance of these experiences she found herself at the door of the blockhouse. To the inmates she appeared as one risen from the dead....It was long before the terrible tidings became an old story in recital, and as for the narrator herself, her long repressed emotions were so completely broken down by the return that to use her own language, she "did nothing but weep for months."

Mrs. Simmons' only sister and husband were killed by Indians in 1813 in one of many raids between Indians and whites. It is a final irony that their bodies were brought to the Simmons' home on the first anniversary of the Dearborn Massacre. Mrs. Simmons raised her sister's children.

Of the seventeen soldiers who survived the ambush and were made prisoners on August 15, 1812, nine survived and were ransomed by a French trader. Only two of the women and two children survived. One was Susan Simmons, the other was Peter Bell.

James Van Horne, Soldier and Prisoner

One of the members of the garrison was James Van Horne, who wrote an account of the massacre and of his captivity five years after his experience. This little book, published in Middlebury, Vermont in 1817, was found behind the wall of a library in a pile of rubble. The Middlebury copy, number 114 of 250 that were printed, is believed to be the only one to survive.

Source: James Van Horne, *Narrative of the Captivity and Sufferings of James Van Horne, Who Was Nine Months a Prisoner by the Indians on the Plains of Michigan*, Middlebury, Vermont, 1817, pp. 3-18.

In the evening of that day, a part of the same tribe came to the encampment with three men, one woman and three children, prisoners.

After having prepared their encamping ground and made fires, they opened a bag and took out two men's hearts and some of the flesh of their breasts. They hung up the two hearts over the fire to dry; then one of them took a piece of the flesh and broiled and ate, and feeling of my breast made motions to the other Indians that a piece of it would be good to eat....

When we stopped at night, I was compelled to prepare the camp. Being much fatigued and hungry, having eaten nothing for three days, and having marched all that time through the Prairie where the grass was as high as my shoulders — I was weak and faint and could not go fast,....

(August) On the 19th we set out again, the storm still continuing and they made me carry all the baggage. The next day we arrived at the village; I was almost dead from hunger, and they gave me some corn.

(September) On the 12th,...They stripped me of my clothes, rubbed my skin over with a yellow clay, pulled out my beard and shaved off all my hair. This was done to make me resemble the Indians in color.

(October) On the 27th the Indian I belonged to, started a north west course. The day was very cold, and I suffered much from hunger....

(November) On the 14th we marched a north course, and at night encamped, where we remained until the 2d of December; during which time we killed a great many deer and raccoon, and found a plenty of wild honey. Here I fared very well....

(December) On the 14th, the tribe to which I belonged went to the banks of Fox River, where all the rest of the tribes assembled for war. There I found some of my fellow prisoners, men and women and was very glad to see them, for I expected they had been killed. I went into one of the cabins, where I found one of the women, and asked her where her child was, she told me the Indians tied it to a tree on the 4th of December because it cried after her for something to eat, and it froze to death.

The Indians held a council of war on the banks of Fox river, and on the 18th all started for Detroit, leaving the prisoners in the care of the old men and squaws. During their absence we almost starved. ...On the 29th, some of the warriors returned from the battle of the River Raisin, bringing a great number of scalps as trophies of victory. As they came in they gave them to me and asked if I knew Them; I told them no. From the great number of scalps I supposed they had penetrated far into the interior of the States. On the 6th of Feb. they held their war dance, over the scalps and hearts. On the 7th, the Indian that I belonged to, packed up a heavy load and told me I must march to the sugar camp. The load was so heavy that I could not stir, and he drew his club and knocked me down, which made two severe wounds on my head. My load was lightened....

On the 8th (of April) I was packed off with fur, to the French traders, where I arrived on the 10th: They were traders whom I knew. I begged of one of them to buy me from the Indian: He told me the British General Proctor had sent a proclamation to the Indians to send all the prisoners to Detroit; but gave me his word that if the Indians did not take me to Detroit, he would do all he could to get me clear....

On the 6th of May the trader's brother came to the village and told the Indians to bring the prisoners to Chicago, for he had received orders from the Great Father, meaning the British King, to buy all the prisoners....We arrived at Chicago on the 12th....

The Humiliation of the Surrender of Detroit

William Hull was the governor of Michigan Territory and a veteran of the American Revolution. Although he was sixty years old and had suffered a stroke, in this campaign Hull led 2,000 regulars and militia through the wilderness in bad weather to the shores of Lake Erie. By the time he reached the lake, on June 29, 1812 so many of his men were sick that he had to hire a ship to transport them on the last part of their journey, a distance of about seventy miles.

Unfortunately, he put his military plans and a list of his men aboard. Unbeknownst to him, on June 18, 1812, war was declared by the United States on Britain (only eleven days before). The British, however, did know of the war. American merchants in business with Canadians sent news to Montreal, where it had been received on June 24. On June 25, Generals Prevost in Quebec and Brock in York received the news; on June 28, Lt. Col. Thomas St. George at Fort Malden was informed, and on July 8, Capt. Charles Roberts at Fort St. Joseph on the eastern end of Lake Superior was told of the declaration of war. So, when Hull's hired ship set sail, the British were waiting. The ship was captured, the strategic plans and the list of soldiers were found and given to General Brock.

Hull's original plan was to capture Fort Malden before moving East. But instead of attacking before the Canadian militia and Indians arrived to strengthen Fort Malden, Hull waited — waited for his men to recover; waited for the wheeled carriages for the cannon; and waited for supplies which had to come the long and precarious route.

Hull sent letters to the Secretary of War in Washington, D.C., and to the governors of Ohio and Kentucky, asking for reinforcements; he talked of his fear of an Indian attack. The letters were sent under a guard of two hundred men who were to escort a supply column from Ohio. On the way back, at Brownstown, on the west side of Lake Erie, the men were ambushed by Tecumseh and a party of his warriors.

Ambushed

The following passage was taken from the journal of an eyewitness of the ambush, Thomas Vercheres de Boucherville, a young man who was living in Amherstburg, Ontario. The month before, a band of Indians led by Tecumseh went to de Boucherville's store and invited him to accompany them on a raid. He went with them, since he felt that he could not refuse them, but was horrified by the ferocity of the attack. "Yet," he says, "I must admit that the heart soon becomes hardened when these bloody scenes are repeated; this I learned when I engaged in similar excursions later on."

Source: Thomas Vercheres de Boucherville, *War on the Detroit: The Chronicles of Thomas Vercheres de Boucherville and The Capitulation by an Ohio Volunteer*, Lakeside Press, Chicago, 1940, pp. 88-90.

We had been preceded on the evening of our arrival at Brownstown by a band of Shawnees and Ottawas who had been sent by Superintendent Elliott to reconnoiter the American position at River Raisin. They told us that they had seen wagons loaded with provisions for Hull's army at Detroit, which was in need of stores of all kinds. Pressed by hunger, Hull that same day sent a body of cavalry to meet the reinforcement that was coming to him and of which he stood in such need, but it had been attacked by our Indians that afternoon between Brownstown and Monguagon. According to their custom they formed an ambush on each side of the road which Hull had opened for the passage of his army through the dense forest and the American troops fell into the trap. Arrows and musket balls rained upon them from every side, sowing death and creating a panic in the ranks easy to understand....The carnage which the Indians perpetrated in this encounter was horrible. They scalped everyone they could overtake and placed these trophies of their bravery on long poles which they stuck up in the ground by the roadside. They also drove long stakes through the bodies of the slain, which were left lying thus exposed. It was a hideous sight to see and little calculated to encourage the enemy when passing by it on the way to Detroit.

Detroit

On August 15, Brock demanded immediate surrender, which was refused, as he had expected. Brock marched his men into the open where he could see cannoneers awaiting a signal to commence firing. Tecumseh had his warriors appear to be a force of 2,000 to 3,000, by having them running past two or three times.

Major-General Brock described the situation himself in his report to Sir George Prevost. Here are excerpts from that report which was written at Detroit on August 17, 1812.

Source: Canadian Archives, Q 118, Ottawa, Ontario, p. 228.

I crossed the river with an intention of waiting in a strong position the effect of our fire upon the Enemy's Camp, and in the hope of compelling him to meet us in the field. But receiving information upon landing that Colonel McArthur, an Officer of high reputation, had left the Garrison three days before with a detachment of five hundred men, and hearing soon afterwards that his Cavalry had been seen that morning three miles in our rear, I decided on an immediate attack....Brig. genl. Hull however prevented this movement by proposing a cessation of hostilities, for the purpose of preparing terms of Capitulation....

On August 16, 1812, the old, sick, frightened Hull surrendered without consulting his officers. He gave up everything — the fort, the garrison, 2,200 men (of whom 600 were regulars), 35 cannon, 2,500 muskets, and 500 rifles.

Campaign Mishandled by General Hull

Brigadier General Robert Lucas was a member of the Ohio Militia until his appointment as a captain in the regular army, (he was later the first governor of Ohio). It was largely due to his report that General Hull was put on trial. The following excerpts from a copy of a letter in Robert Lucas' journal reveal the terrible frustration that he and other officers and men felt at the ineptitude and mishandling of the campaign by General Hull. It also shows that the Indians were not the only ones who returned with trophies.

Source: Robert Lucas, *The Robert Lucas Journal of The War of 1812 During The Campaign Under General William Hull*, edited by John C. Parish, State Historical Society of Iowa, Iowa City, 1906, pp. 59-61.

Detroit

12 August 1812

Dear Sir, I have the mortification to announce to you, that on the evening of the 7th inst[a]nt while waiting with anxiety for liberty to march to Maldon, that the American Army was ordered by their Genl to recross the river to Detroit,...and must now be sunk into Disgrace for the want of a General at their head —

...neither was there ever men of talents as they are so shamefully opposed by an imbesile or Treacherous commander as they have been — ...Would to God Either of our Colonels had the command, if they had, we might yet wipe of[f] the foul stain, that has been brought upon us. We are now reduced to a perilous situation, the British are reinforcing, our Communication[s] with the States are cut of[f], our Provisions growing short, and likely to be Surrounded by hosts of Savages....

With Sentiments of respect I am your obed[i]ent servant,

Robert Lucas

This Afternoon Colo Miller returned with his detachment after undergoing a fateegue of a Severe engagement, and being kep[t] for Several days without Provisions or Tents. Some of them had Indian Scalps hanging to the ramrods of their muskets as they marched in —

Hull Court-martialed

Hull was taken prisoner to York. Later he was court-martialed on charges of treason, and was found guilty of cowardice and neglect of duty. During the testimony it was revealed that instead of planning with his staff, he sat in his tent, alone, chewing tobacco. He has the dubious distinction of being the only American officer to surrender an American city to a foreign force.

Here are excerpts of the trial of General Hull:

Source: Lieutenant Colonel Forbes of the forty-second regt., U. S. Infantry, and a supernumerary Member of the Court, *Report of The Trial of Brig. General William Hull; Commanding the North-Western Army of the United States, by a Court Martial Held at Albany on Monday, 3d January, 1814 and Succeeding Days*, Eastburn, Kirk, and Co., New York, 1814, p. 118.

Saturday morning, March 26, 1814 — the court met...and after due consideration, do sentence him to be shot to death, two thirds of the court concurring in the sentence.

The court in consideration of Brigadier General Hull's revolutionary services, and his advanced age, earnestly recommend him to the mercy of the President of the United States.

April, 1814 — The sentence of the court is approved and the execution of remitted.

By directions of the court-martial the president gave the following directions to General Hull:

Albany, March 28, 1814.

Sir — You will please to return to your usual place of residence in Massachusetts — and there continue until you shall receive orders from the president of the United States. Your humble servant.

Queenston Heights - The Niagara Campaign

Major General Stephen Van Rensselaer, a large landowner with no military experience, was in charge of the Niagara Campaign. Plans called for taking two British forts; Fort Erie, where Lake Erie flows into the Niagara River, and Fort George, where the Niagara River enters Lake Ontario. Niagara Falls is between the two Great Lakes. Queenston is not far from Fort George.

Where Are the Oars? Where Are the Boats?

October 13, 1812

Excerpts from Van Rensselaer's official report to Major General Dearborn show his desperation and humiliation at the disastrous results of his campaign to invade Canada. The war was becoming one blunder after another.

Source: John Brannan, editor, *Official Letters of the Military and Naval Officers of the United States, During the War with Great Britain in the Years 1812,13,14, and 15*, Arno Press & *The New York Times*. Reprint edition 1971, originally published by Way & Gideon, Washington City, 1823, pp .75-78.

The attack was to have been made at 4 o'clock in the morning of the 11th, by crossing over in boats at the Old Ferry opposite the heights. To avoid any embarrassment in crossing the river, (which is here a sheet of violent eddies) experienced boatmen were procured to take the boats from the landing below to the place of embarkation. Lieutenant Sim was considered the man of greatest skill for this service. He went ahead, and in the extreme darkness, passed the intended place far up the river; and there in a most extraordinary manner, fastened his boat to the shore, and abandoned the detachment. In his front boat he had carried nearly every oar which was prepared for all the boats. In this agonizing dilemma, stood officers and men, whose ardor had not been cooled by exposure through the night to one of the most tremendous north-east storms, which continued, unabated, for twenty-eight hours, and deluged the whole camp. The approach of day-light extinguished every prospect of success, and the detachment returned to camp....

...now determined to attack Queenstown, I sent new orders to general Smyth to march; Every precaution was now adopted as to boats, and the most confidential and experienced men to manage them....

At dawn of day the boats were in readiness, and the troops commenced embarking, under the cover of a commanding battery....

The boats were somewhat embarrassed with the eddies, as well as with a shower of shot: but colonel Van Rensselaer, with about 100 men, soon effected his landing amidst a tremendous fire directed upon him from every point: but to the astonishment of all who witnessed the scene, this van of the column advanced slowly against the fire. It was a serious misfortune...that in a few minutes after landing, colonel Van Rensselaer received four wounds. A ball passed through his right thigh, entering just below the hip bone; another shot passed through the same thigh, a little below; the third through the calf of his leg; and a fourth contused his heel. This was quite a crisis in the expedition. Under so severe a fire it was difficult to form raw troops. By some mismanagement of the boatmen, lieutenant colonel Chrystie did not arrive until some time after this, and was wounded in the hand in passing the river....

For some time after I had passed over, the victory seemed complete;....But very soon the enemy was reinforced by a detachment of several hundred Indians from Chippawa — they commenced a furious attack, but were promptly met and routed by the rifle and bayonet. By this time I perceived my troops were embarking very slowly. I passed immediately over to accelerate their movements; but to my utter astonishment, I found at the very moment when complete victory was in our hands, the ardor of the unengaged troops had entirely subsided. I rode in all directions — urged men by every consideration to pass over, but in vain.

Finding to my infinite mortification, that no reinforcement would pass over; seeing that another severe conflict must soon commence; and knowing that the brave men on the heights were quite exhausted and nearly out of ammunition, all I could do was to send them a fresh supply of cartridges. At this critical moment I despatched a note to general Wadsworth, acquainting him with our situation — leaving the course to be pursued much to his own judgment, with assurance, that if he thought best to retreat, I would endeavour to send as many boats as I could command, and cover his retreat, by every fire I could safely make. But the boats were dispersed — many of the boatmen had fled, panic struck, and but few got off.

...The enemy succeeded in repossessing their battery; and gaining advantage on every side, the brave men who had gained the victory, exhausted of strength and ammunition, and grieved at the unpardonable neglect of their fellow-soldiers, gave up the conflict.

I can only add, that the victory was really won; but lost for the want of a small reinforcement. One-third part of the idle men might have saved all....

I have reason to believe that many of our troops fled to the woods, with the hope of crossing the river, I have not been able to learn the probable number of killed, wounded and prisoners. The slaughter of our troops must have been very considerable. And the enemy have suffered severely.

General Brock is among their slain, and his aid-de-camp mortally wounded.

Even surrendering was difficult! Gen. Winfield Scott decided to surrender to British regulars rather than to face a massacre by Indian allies of the British. Two men that he sent carrying flags of truce were killed by Indians on their way to the British. Scott himself, carrying his sword high with a fellow officer's white cravat tied to it, went toward the British lines. He was surrounded by Indians and would also have been killed except for the timely intervention of a twenty-one-year-old law student, a member of the York Volunteers. John Beverley Robinson (who was later named Attorney-General of Canada) took Scott through to the British where his surrender was accepted.

British regulars, the Lincoln and York Militia, Indians, and a platoon of former runaway slaves, won the Battle of Queenston Heights. Nine hundred American men surrendered. Five hundred were killed or wounded. British and Indians suffered only nineteen killed and seventy-seven wounded.

A critical factor was the presence of John Norton, a Mohawk chief who led 250 warriors behind the American lines. The sight of these men — painted for war, and their blood-curdling war whoops, terrorized the poorly-trained American militia. With Norton was John Brant, the eighteen-year-old son of Joseph Brant who had fought for the British in the Revolutionary War.

The Battle of Queenston

John Norton was the son of a Cherokee father and a Scottish mother. Well educated, he spoke English, French, German, Spanish, and twelve Indian languages. In 1803, he went to Britain on behalf of the Grand River Indians. He became a celebrity, making friends with important people in London and Cambridge. The Duke of Northumberland took on the responsibility of getting Norton's book, History of the Confederate Tribes & Memoirs of the late Military Operations in Canada, *published in England. For many years Norton kept a journal. The last two hundred pages of it are about the War of 1812, and are generally considered to be the most accurate eyewitness account. Following are excerpts from Norton's entries about the Battle of Queenston.*

Source: Major John Norton, *The Journal of Major John Norton, 1816*, The Champlain Society, Toronto, 1970, pp. 304-312.

At this time, the number of my Men was considerably reduced, — a great part had gone home, — the approach of Winter made them feel the Want of Warm Clothing, and in constant Marching they had worn out their Mocasins. The fall of the Leaf, the season for hunting the Buck, had arrived, & many had gone to the Woods, to supply their Wants by the Chase: — few would have remained, had not the Love of Glory animated their hearts,...while they awaited the coming of the Enemy. There were then hardly Three Hundred Warriors remaining at Niagara.

On the Morning of the 13, a firing was heard from Queenstown, ...The Canonade had commenced, which roused the spirits of the Warriors, & shouts re-echoed from one to another. All ran towards Queenstown....

We discovered only a few Militia Men that had escaped from Queenstown, — they said in excuse for their flight, that Six thousand Americans had gained possession of Queenstown Heights; — some Warriors answered, — "The more game the better hunting." These reports however had not the same effect upon all, — many were alarmed thereby, and filled with anxiety for the safety of their families, which at that time happened to be at Niagara; — we found ourselves much diminished in number by the imperceptible desertion of many; — there did not remain together more than Eighty Men...

When we saw the right Wing enter the Field, — we rushed forward, — the enemy fired, — we closed & they ran; — from the Side of a Hill where they lay, they fired again, — we came in upon them Swiftly; — they left their Cannon, & we raised the Shout of Victory. Whilst our Cannon fired on the right, we were in rear of their Centre, (which lined the Skirts of the field, through which our right Wing was advancing); — It fell into confusion, — they ran in disorder, — many falling on the way....We rushed forward,...the Enemy disappeared under the Bank; many plunging into the River. The inconsiderate still continued to fire at them, until checked by repeated commands of "Stop fire." The White flag from the American General then met General Sheaffe, proposing to Surrender at Discretion the remainder of those who had invaded us. The Prisoners amounted to about Nine Hundred; — among these were General Wadsworth, Colonels Scot, Christie and many others. They had no reason to complain of cruelty this day....

...it was generally allowed that twenty two hundred Men had crossed the river: — it was reported that 4000 Men including Militia had been in readiness at Lewistown, — but that the Militia in the rear becoming disheartened at the incessant attacks upon those who had already passed to the Canadian Shore, and the havock made among them, (which they perceived by the return of the dead & wounded in the Boats intended for their Transportation, — they refused to embark, — and it was to remove this panic, that General Van Ransailler returned to Lewistown, — but all his endeavours were ineffectual: — prior to our final assault, many of the Enemy had recrossed!

The grief caused by the Loss of General Brock threw a gloom over the sensations which this brilliant Success might have raised. The dead of the Enemy were buried, and we collected the remains of our gallant friends: — They were interred with the due honours. At the Funeral of General Brock, a great proportion of the Militia of the Country attended, (having been called upon to assemble) — & a General Salute was also given from the cannon in the Enemy's Garrison, immediately after our cannon had fired.

In a council, General Sheaffe expressed to the Five Nations, in the Warmest Manner, his thanks for their Spirited Exertions. A Truce was agreed upon, & all the Militia, taken in the late conflict, were allowed to return home, in the same manner as had been done in the capture of General Hull, only, — the Regular Troops taken prisoners, were sent to Quebec....

Every few days, we gained some intelligence through the means of Deserters that were constantly coming to us. We got Smyth's Proclamation, which even exceeded Hulls'; — in it, he offers a reward of forty Dollars for the despoils [scalp] of ev'ry Indian Warrior.

The Battle of Queenston (Canadian National Archives)

Laura Secord and Beaver Dams

Laura Secord's name and face are familiar to Canadians; since 1913 Laura Secord has been used as the brand name for a kind of fine chocolates (and her picture is on the box). She became a Canadian folk hero, not because of the candy named for her, but because of a courageous walk she took over hazardous terrain in June of 1813.

The Secords were living on a grant of land in the Niagara region, which was at that time held by the Americans. Mrs. Secord overheard some American officers discussing a plan to attack the 49th British Regiment under the command of James Fitzgibbon.

Mr. Secord had commanded a company of militia in the battle of Queenston and may have been wounded there. In any case, he was so incapacitated that he could not make the journey himself to warn Fitzgibbon of the impending attack. The couple agreed that Laura must go.

The Secord story has taken on almost mythical qualities and has gained many embellishments over the years. Sometimes Laura is called "the lady with the cow" because one version has her leading a cow through enemy lines to avoid suspicion. Another has her walking barefoot over rough terrain, while her obituary has her making the trip at night — a journey that would be virtually impossible for even the most able woodsman.

Mrs. Secord herself never made any of these claims.

In 1861, Benson J. Lossing received a letter from Mrs. Secord. He was gathering material for his book, The Pictorial Field-Book of the War of 1812 *and had asked her for an account of her famous adventure. When Lossing received her reply, Laura Secord was ninety-two years old, still in full command of her faculties, and able to read without glasses. She was living in the small Canadian village of Chippewa on the Niagara River, not far from the site of the events she related in her letter.*

Following are excerpts from Laura Secord's letter to Lossing:

Source: George Coventry Papers, MG 24, K2, vol. 13, National Archives of Canada, pp. 396-398.

After going to St. David's, and the recovery of Mr. Secord, we returned again to Queenston, where my courage again was much tried. It was then I gained the secret plan laid to capture Captain Fitzgibbon and his party. I was determined, if possible, to save them. I had much difficulty in getting through the American guards. They were ten miles out in the country. When I came to a field belonging to a Mr. DeCou, in the neighborhood of Beaver Dams, I then had walked nineteen miles. By that time daylight had left me. I had yet a swift stream of water to cross over an old fallen tree [Twelve-mile Creek], and to climb a high hill, which fatigued me very much.

Before I arrived at the encampment of the Indians, as I approached they all arose with one of their war-yells, which indeed awed me. You may imagine what my feelings were to behold so many savages. With forced courage I went to one of the chiefs, told him I had great news for his commander, and that he must take me to him, or they would be all lost. He did not understand me, but said, "Woman! what does woman want here?" The scene by moonlight might have been grand, but to a weak woman certainly terrifying. With difficulty I got one of the chiefs to go with me to their commander. With the intelligence I gave him he formed his plans and saved his country. I have ever found the brave and noble Colonel Fitzgibbon a friend to me; may he prosper in the world to come as he has done in this.

Laura Secord
Chippewa, U. C. February 18, 1861

On June 23, 1813, 500 Americans marched to Queenston intending to surprise and capture Fitzgibbon and his men.

The Americans were ambushed in thick woods by about 300 Indians from Quebec and 100 Mohawks. For over three hours the Americans fought desperately. They were terrified of having to surrender to the Indians. Fitzgibbon heard the shooting and went to the scene with reinforcements. The Americans willingly surrendered to him.

*The De Cou's house where Laura Secord gave Fitzgibbon
the news of the planned attack. (National Archives of Canada.)*

*Fitzgibbon made a statement about the episode in which he gave great credit
to Mrs. Secord. It is signed, "James Fitzgibbon, formerly lieutenant in the Forty-
ninth Regiment." The original was sent to Mrs. Secord.*

Source: Mary Agnes Fitzgibbon, *A Veteran of 1812, The Life of James Fitzgibbon*, William
Briggs, Toronto, 1898, p. 84.

I do hereby certify that Mrs. Secord, wife of James Secord, of
Chippewa, Esq., did, in the month of June, 1813, walk from her
house, near the village of St. David's, to De Cou's house in Thorold
by a circuitous route of about twenty miles, partly through the woods,
to acquaint me that the enemy intended to attempt, by surprise, to
capture a detachment of the 49 Regiment, then under my command, she having obtained such knowledge from good authority,
as the event proved. Mrs. Secord was a person of slight and delicate
frame, and made the effort in weather excessively warm, and I
dreaded at the time that she must suffer in health in consequence of
fatigue and anxiety, she having been exposed to danger from the
enemy, through whose lines of communication she had to pass.

The attempt was made on my detachment by the enemy; and his detachment, consisting of upwards of 500 men and a field-piece and 50 dragoons, were captured in consequence.

Beaver Dams, as this battle is known, was a blow to American morale. What should have been little more than a raid, turned into another humiliating defeat. There is no doubt that Laura Secord played a significant part in the Canadian victory.

When the Prince of Wales was making a tour of Canada in 1860, Mrs. Secord applied for permission to add her name to a list of soldiers who had served on the Niagara Frontier during the War of 1812. Naturally, the request was met with surprise, but, upon hearing an account of Laura Secord's journey, her name was placed on the list with other veterans. The story was brought to the attention of the Prince, who was so impressed that he sent a gift of 100 pounds sterling to be formally presented to her.

Two monuments have been erected in her honor by the Canadian government, and her portrait hangs in Parliament Building, in Ottawa, Ontario, the capital of Canada.

Battle of Thames, The Death of Tecumseh

The Battle of the Thames.

Colonel Henry Proctor and his men at Fort Malden (near present day Windsor, Ontario) was at the end of a long, weak supply-line and his supplies were running short. He decided to move up the Thames River to join British Brigadier General John Vincent's army at Burlington, Ontario. Proctor left Fort Malden on September 27, 1813 and was pursued by William Henry Harrison. Proctor's men were sick and exhausted. Their retreat had become disorganized. Harrison was getting closer and was being joined by support groups so that he had a force of about 3,500 men.

He caught up with the British and Indians on the banks of the Thames, where he defeated them. Tecumseh was killed during the fierce hand-to-hand fighting, but his body was never found.

After Tecumseh's death, tribes returned to their old conflicts amongst themselves, further weakening their efforts to stop the American westward movement. In the loss of a strong leader the Indians lost their last real chance for an Indian state.

"Where the hopes of the Red Man perished"

Shortly before the battle which took place on October 5, 1813, Tecumseh made a speech to Col. Proctor, who, at that time, was in charge of about 800 to 1,000 Indians and 900 soldiers (about only half of them were well enough to fight). The Shawnee chief spoke of empty promises, and of being left out of planning sessions. He chided Proctor for his lack of bravery and stated his determination "...to defend our lands..." and, if necessary, to die there. The speech was found with Col. Proctor's papers which were taken by Harrison after the battle. It is dated Amherstburg, September 18th, 1813.

Source: *America; Great Crises in Our History Told By Its Makers, op. cit.,* pp. 187-189.

Father, listen to your children! you have them now all before you. The war before this our British father gave the hatchet to his red children, when old chiefs were alive. They are now dead. In that war our father was thrown on his back by the Americans, and our father took them by the hand without our knowledge; and we are afraid that our father will do so again at this time.

Summer before last, when I came forward with my red brethren, and was ready to take up the hatchet in favor of our British father, we were told not to be in a hurry, that he had not yet determined to fight the Americans.

Listen! When war was declared, our father stood up and gave us the tomahawk, and told us that he was ready to strike the Americans; that he wanted our assistance, and that he would certainly get us our lands back, which the Americans had taken from us.

Listen! You told us, at that time, to bring forward our families to this place, and we did so: — and you promised to take care of them, and that they should want for nothing, while the men would go and fight the enemy. That we need not trouble ourselves about the enemy's garrisons that we knew nothing about them, and that our father would attend to that part of the business. You also told your red children that you would take good care of your garrison here, which made our hearts glad.

Listen! When we were last at the Rapids, it is true we gave you little assistance. It is hard to fight people who live like ground-hogs.

Father, listen!...we were much astonished to see our father tying up everything and preparing to run away the other, without letting his red children know what his intentions are. You always told us to remain here and take care of our lands. It made our hearts glad to hear that was your wish. Our great father, the King, is the head, and you represent him. You always told us that you would never draw your foot off British ground; but now, father, we see you are drawing back, and we are sorry to see our father doing so without seeing the enemy. We must compare our father's conduct to a fat animal that carried its tail upon its back, but when affrighted, it drops it between its legs and runs off.

Listen, Father! The Americans have not yet defeated us by land; neither are we sure that they have done so by water — we therefore wish to remain here and fight our enemy, should they make their appearance. If they defeat us, we will then retreat with our father.

At the battle of the Rapids, last war, the Americans certainly defeated us; and when we retreated to our father's fort in that place, the gates were shut against us. —We were afraid that it would now be the case, but instead of that, we now see our British father preparing to march out of his garrison.

Father! You have got the arms and ammunition which our great father sent for his red children. If you have an idea of going away, give them to us, and you may go and welcome, for us. Our lives are in the hands of the Great Spirit. We are determined to defend our lands, and if it is his will, we wish to leave our bones upon them.

Tecumseh

Tecumseh

Since 1805, Tecumseh, the Shawnee chief, and his brother, The Prophet, had been trying to create an Indian confederacy of all the tribes in the areas south and west of Lake Erie, where settlers were encroaching on Indian land. In this effort they had the support of the British government. An Indian buffer state would discourage large numbers of Americans from moving into Canada — so many that the British government in Canada feared a movement to add Canada to the United States. Fur traders agreed that American movements west should be stopped as they depended on Indians for their furs.

Tecumseh did not want to be dependent on the British, but Indians needed goods and arms that the British were willing to supply. Therefore, he felt that they needed to help the British against the Americans.

Tecumseh and General Isaac Brock only met once, but each recognized the greatness of the other. Tecumseh's impression of Brock was "This is a man." Their admiration was mutual. Brock wrote:

Source: William Wood, editor, *Select British Documents of the Canadian War of 1812,* Brock to Lord Liverpool, 29 August, Toronto, vol. I, p. 508.

He who attracted most my attention was a Shawnee chief, Tecumseh...a more sagacious or a more gallant warrior does not I believe exist. He has the admiration of everyone who conversed with him.

Following is an excerpt from a tribute to the dead warrior, written by an unknown author. The second line haunts with its truth. When Tecumseh died, the hopes of the Indians died with him.

Source: Burton Egbert Stevenson, editor, *Poems of American History,* pp. 306.

Gloom, silence, and solitude rest on the spot
   Where the hopes of the red man perished;
But the fame of the hero who fell shall not,
   By the virtuous, cease to be cherished.

The Battle of Crysler's Farm

John Crysler was a prosperous farmer with land along the St. Lawrence River near Prescott, Ontario. Early in October of 1813, the American Major General James Wilkinson arrived at Sackets Harbor from the Niagara Frontier. Having given up his plans to attack Kingston, Ontario because it was too fortified, Wilkinson decided to open a campaign against Montreal. With 8,000 men in boats, he moved down river, not expecting any enemy action. But Canadian militia had responded to a call and harassed Americans from the riverbank. Wilkinson was forced to off-load 2,500 men to drive off their assailants and to protect the boats when they went through the treacherous Long Sault (pronounced Long Sue) Rapids.

When Wilkinson found that in addition to the militia shooting at his men along the riverbank, there were forces pursuing him (630 regulars and a tiny fleet, gunboats, bateaux and two schooners), he sent another 2,000 regulars to serve as a rear guard.

The Invasion Fails

The enemies met at Mr. Crysler's farm on November 11, 1813. The Americans were badly led and ill-trained, two factors which turned the attempted invasion into a rout.

Two days later, an unnamed American soldier wrote of the behavior of the men:

Source: M. Zaslow, editor, *The Defended Border, Upper Canada and the War of 1812*, Toronto, 1964, p. 81.

Our troops retreated with great precipitation to the boats, and crossed the river, leaving the British on the field....What appears extraordinary in this affair is that nearly 1000 of our troops crossed to the American side during the engagement!

This probably means that they bolted and ran or deserted.

The Defeat of the Creek Indians
Fort Mims, Alabama

When Tecumseh was in the South, trying to organize Indian tribes against the Americans, one of those who heard him was a Creek chief, Red Eagle. He had been named William Weatherford by his Scottish father. In August 1813, he made a surprise raid on Fort Mims, Alabama, killing 250 whites. Many others were burned to death inside buildings torched by the "Red Sticks". (Creeks carried red clubs and so they became known as Red Sticks.) The United States immediately sent in troops to stop any further uprisings. Major General Andrew Jackson of the Tennessee militia quickly raised 2,000 volunteers and by forced marches soon reached and destroyed the Creek stronghold, Tallushatchee. Jackson chased Red Eagle and wiped out all resistance, killing nearly 1,000 Creeks. He forced the Creeks to forfeit their traditional lands to the United States, and to leave the area.

"The enemy fought with savage fury"

John Coffee, Brigadier General of Cavalry and Riflemen on the staff of General Andrew Jackson, in an official report, gave an account of the part his men played in the campaign. He spoke almost reverently of the bravery of the warriors who fought to the very last man that terrible day, November 4, 1813.

Source: Brannan, ed., *Official Letters of the Military and Naval Officers, op. cit.*, pp. 255-256.

Pursuant to your order of the 2d, I detailed from my brigade of cavalry and mounted riflemen, 900 men and officers, and proceeding directly to the Tallushatchee towns....I arrived within one and a half miles of the town on the morning of the 3d, at which place I divided my detachment into two columns, the right composed of the cavalry commanded by Colonel Allcorn, to cross over a large creek that lay between us and the towns: the left column was of the mounted riflemen, under the command of colonel Cannon, with whom I marched myself. Colonel Allcorn was ordered to march up on the right, and encircle one half of the town, and at the same time the left would form a half circle on the left, and unite the head of the columns in front of the town: all of which was performed as I could wish. When I arrived within half a mile of the town, the drums of the enemy began to beat, mingled with their savage yells, preparing for action. It was after sun-rise an hour, when the action was brought on by captain Hammond and lieutenant Patterson's companies, who had gone on within the circle of alignment, for the purpose of drawing out the enemy from their buildings, which had the most happy effect. As soon as captain Hammond exhibited his front in view of the town, (which stood in open woodland) and gave a few scattering shot, the enemy formed and made a violent charge on him: he gave way as they advanced, until they met our right column, which gave them a general fire, and then charged; this changed the direction of the charge completely; the enemy retreated firing, until they got around, and in their buildings, where they made all the resistance that an overpowered soldier could do; they fought as long as one existed, but their destruction was very soon completed; our men rushed up to the doors of the houses, and in a few minutes killed the last warrior of them; the enemy fought with savage fury, and met death with all its horrors, without shrinking or complaining; not one asked to be spared, but fought as long as they could stand or sit. In consequence of their flying to their houses and mixing with the families, our men, in killing the males, without intention killed and wounded a few of the squaws and children, which was regretted by every officer and soldier of the detachment, but which could not be avoided.

The number of the enemy killed, was 186 that were counted, and a number of others that were killed in the weeds not found. I think the calculation a reasonable one, to say 200 of them were killed, and 84 prisoners, of women and children, were taken; not one of the warriors escaped to carry the news, a circumstance unknown heretofore.

We lost five men killed, and 41 wounded, none mortally, the greater part slightly, a number with arrows: this appears to form a very principal part of the enemy's arms for warfare, every man having a bow with a bundle of arrows, which is used after the first fire with the gun, until a leisure time for leading offers.

It is with pleasure I say, that our men acted with deliberation and firmness; notwithstanding our numbers were superior to that of the enemy, it was a circumstance to us unknown, and from the parade of the enemy, we had every reason to suppose them our equals in number: but there appeared no visible traces of alarm in any, but on the contrary, all appeared cool and determined, and no doubt when they face a foe of their own, or superior number, they will show the same courage as on this occasion.

"The power of the Creeks is I think forever crushed"

There were three battles. After the Battle of Horseshoe Bend on the Tallapoosa River, on March 28, 1814, Jackson made his official report, in which he stated his intention to completely crush the Creek nation.

Source: *America; Great Crises in our History, op. cit.* pp. 238-240.

Determined to exterminate them,…

....

The enemy was completely routed. Five hundred and fifty-seven were left dead on the peninsula, and a great number were killed by the horsemen in attempting to cross the river. It is believed that not more than twenty have escaped.

The fighting continued with some severity about five hours, but we continued to destroy many of them, who had concealed themselves under the banks of the river, until we were prevented by the night. This morning we killed sixteen who had been concealed. We took about 250 prisoners, all women and children except two or three. Our loss is 106 wounded, and 25 killed.

The power of the Creeks is I think forever crushed.

The Battle of Lundy's Lane

Lundy's Lane was a road near a spot where the Chippewa River empties into the Niagara River. It is between Fort Erie and Queenston, near the Great Falls. The road joins another road extending from Chippewa to Queenston. This area on the Niagara Frontier was in Canada.

The battle did not begin until sunset and went on into the night. British and American troops mistook each other in the darkness. The British commander, Major Phineas Riall, was lost and captured along with several other officers and staff. Finally, General Brown ordered a young officer to storm the hill and take it. Colonel Miller, with fewer than 300 men, overcame the gunners, using the light of their matches to find their targets. Without cannon, the British were forced to give up the hill.

Brigadier General Eleazar Ripley became commander after Brown was wounded twice, and taken from the field. Contrary to Brown's orders, Ripley did not return to take the cannon and secure the territory they had captured during the night in the fiercest battle of the war. In the morning Ripley and his army again crossed the Chippewa River only to find that the British had retaken the high ground above Lundy's Lane.

Lundy's Lane was the most costly battle of the war. Nearly 1,000 Americans were killed, wounded or captured. British losses were about the same.

Lundy's Lane halted Brown's invasion of Upper Canada. Ripley was removed from his command, but the damage was already done. His delay had cost the Americans the victory, but his poor judgment did not stop there. After Brown was put on a boat and taken to Buffalo, Ripley destroyed all the defenses, the bridge, even some American supplies. He took his army to Fort Erie, where defenses were being strengthened against an expected British attack.

"So awful a night"

John Le Couteur was a young lieutenant from the Channel Island of Jersey. He served with the 104th Foot and he kept a journal during the War of 1812. While he was stationed at Kingston, he enjoyed the social activities there and wrote about his life in a very amusing, light-hearted way. But quite a different tone pervades a letter written to his brother after the battle at Lundy's Lane.

The last sentence of his letter to his brother may be one of the saddest and most naive statements ever made by a soldier.

Source: Donald E. Graves, editor, *Merry Hearts Make Light Days: The War of 1812 Journal of Lt. John Le Couteur*, Carleton University Press, Ottawa, Canada, 1994, pp. 178-179.

My Dear William,...

Until the morning we were not aware of our Victory's being so complete. Near three hundred of the enemy lay dead on the field of battle, besides a great many wounded. Mrs. Willson reckoned Sixty waggon loads of wounded that passed her house, and Thirty officers were in her house early in the action. But our Victory was a (illegible) one. We have Fifty officers killed, wounded and missing, most of them Prisoner, from going in among the enemy in the Dark, and from speaking the same language, once separated we could not distinguish friends from foe. There were (word missing) officers killed and about 18 wounded. Poor Moorson was killed, whilst cheering (words missing) the Royals. Loring was made P(risoner) carrying orders and getting among (words missing) instead of our own troops....The loss among the Troops was (word missing) K(ille)d, 404 w(ounde)d, and 140 missing and Prisoners....

I assure I never passed so awful a night as that of the action. The stillness of the evening after the firing ceased, the Groans of the dying and wounded, I went to several of them and got a Captain taken away. I could not sleep tho' I was quite fatigued and weak from 36 hours marching, fasting and Fighting. I was cold and wretched, what must not have been the misery of those Unfortunates who remained on the field. A Soldier's life is very horrid sometimes.

Battle of Fort Erie

15 August 1814

In 1814, the Americans controlled Lake Erie. Although until July of that year there were no major battles, Americans conducted a series of cruel raids along the Canadian (North) shores of Lake Erie.

In May, July, August, and September, Port Dover alone was raided several times. Homes were robbed, buildings and crops were burned. People were mistreated and taken prisoner. There were even some murders. William H. Merritt wrote about the raids in his journal.

Source: William Wood, editor, *Select Documents of the Canadian War of 1812*, Toronto, 1920-1928, Vol., III, p. 617.

The militia were daily skirmishing and driving in the States' parties, who were plundering every house they could get at: They even plundered women of everything they had.

To make matters worse, many of the raiders were Canadian Volunteers fighting on the side of the Americans. The raids were successful in that Americans were able to carry them out, but they turned Canadians away from their formerly friendly feelings toward Americans.

On July 3rd, 1814, General Jacob Brown captured Fort Erie, and began intensive work to strengthen it. Some military strategists believe that General Gordon Drummond could have captured Fort Erie quite easily if he had moved quickly. However, his troops were exhausted from the fierce fighting at Lundy's Lane, and he needed reinforcements, so it was not until the third of August that he began a siege. Drummond had about 3,000 regulars while the Americans had barely 2,000.

For two days there was a constant barrage of British fire. Early in the morning of the 14th of August, 1814, the British attacked. They were kept at bay on two sides, but one group, headed by Lt. Col. Drummond, the nephew of General Drummond, gained entrance to the bastion. The Americans were able to keep them there, but were not strong enough to drive them out.

"I can blow them all to Hell in a minute"

Jabez Fisk was there that day. In a letter dated 20 May 1863, to Benson J. Lossing, he told of the explosion that ended the battle:

Source: Benson J. Lossing, *The Pictorial Field-Book of the War of 1812*, New York, Harper & Brothers, 1868, p. 94.

Three or four hundred of the enemy had got into the bastion. At this time, an American officer came running up and said, "General Gaines, the bastion is full. I can blow them all to hell in a minute!" They both passed back through a stone building, and in a short time the bastion and the British were high in the air. General Gaines soon returned, swinging his hat, and shouting "Hurrah for Little York!"

(This was a reference to the blowing up of a British magazine at Little York, where General Zebulon Pike was killed.)

British soldiers had been standing over an arsenal of American ammunition when the ground began to shake and rise, then burst open in a terrible explosion. This was followed by heavy artillery fire. The British troops panicked and withdrew, but reorganized and continued the siege.

General Brown, still weak from his wounds, left Batavia, New York, and went to Fort Erie to take command.

On September 17, Americans made a surprise raid on the British, whose numbers had been severely reduced by typhoid fever, other sickness, constant rain, and losses elsewhere. The batteries were taken, British taken prisoner, cannon, cannon carriages, and ammunition destroyed.

Further weakened by the raid, the British gave up and left. On November 5, 1814, the Americans abandoned the fort and blew it up.

In a letter dated 24 September 1814, Joseph Rosseel perceived the battle at Fort Erie to be a turning point in the war.

Source: David Parish Papers, *op. cit.*

Mr. Cleveland just in from the Harbour says he has seen a Letter from Gen. Brown to his Brother mentioning that on the 18th he made a sortie on Gen. Drummond took all his artillerie, 400 prisoners and Killed as many — if this be true there is an end of that army.

Desertion and Mutiny

Soldiers had appalling living conditions, and there was usually a lack of food and supplies. Consequently, desertion and mutiny were constant threats to the officers.

The Soldiers' Life

P. Finan lived on the military post at York, (now Toronto), Ontario with his father. In his memoirs he described, among other things, the harsh treatment of deserters. He believed that extreme sentences were justified to dissuade others from running away.

Source: John Gellner, *op. cit.*, pp. 106-107.

As desertion was very frequent at this time, the Indians were employed to intercept the deserters in the woods, and were allowed a reward for every soldier, dead or alive, they brought into town.

...One man of my father's regiment was found frozen to death at the foot of a small precipice, which, from the appearance of the snow on the side of it, he had frequently attempted to ascend, but had become overpowered by the frost before he could accomplish it. He was suspended during the day to the upper end of a long post, in a conspicuous situation, at the barracks; and the head of one of De Watteville's regiment, brought in at the same time, was placed upon the top of a long pole, in full view of his late comrades. This treatment of the dead bodies of the unfortunate men may, perhaps, appear very barbarous, and unbecoming a British army; but when the pernicious effect of desertion in time of war are taken into consideration, particularly at such a critical period as this was, as the Americans had become very successful in the upper part of the country, and the loss of the men being trifling when compared with the consequences that might result from the enemy being put in possession of the information that deserters might carry to them, the necessity of putting a stop to the baneful practice will be found to have tolerated every method that could be resorted to for that purpose.

A soldier, Elias Darnell, described conditions:

Source: *Ibid.*, pp. 139-141.

16th. We have drawn no flour since the 10th, in consequence of which there was a letter handed to the General last night secretly, which stated that the volunteers in two days, except flour came before that time, would start and go to it; and they would carry their camp equipage to the fort if the General required it. This news was soon circulated through camp. The officers used every argument to suppress the appearance of a mutiny.

17th. Three hundred head of hogs arrived to our relief.

22nd. A little flour came to camp once more; quarter-rations of that article were issued, which was welcomed by rejoicing throughout camp.

24th. Capt. Hickman returned with joyful news — that we should in a short time be supplied with flour....Obstacles had emerged in the path to victory, which must have appeared unsurmountable to every person endowed with common sense. The distance to Canada, the unpreparedness of the army, the scarcity of provisions, and the badness of the weather, show that Malden cannot be taken in the remaining part of our time. And would it not have been better if this army had been disbanded? Our sufferings at this place have been greater than if we had been in a severe battle. More than one hundred lives have been lost, owing to our bad accommodations! The sufferings of about three hundred sick at a time, who are exposed to the cold ground and deprived of every nourishment, are sufficient proofs of our wretched condition!

29th. We are now commencing one of the most serious marches ever performed by the Americans. Destitute, in a measure, of clothes, shoes, and provisions, the most essential articles necessary for the existence and preservation of the human species in this world, and more particularly in this cold climate. Three sleds are prepared for each company, each to be pulled by a packhorse, which has been without food for two weeks except brush, and will not be better fed while in our service; probably the most of these horses never had harness....

Officers were angry and frustrated because their troops were victims of those making a profit from the war. General Jacob Brown complained to James Monroe about the state of the soldiers at Sackets Harbor.

Source: C. Gerard Hoard, *Major General Jacob Jennings Brown*, Hungerford-Holbrook, Watertown, New York, 1979, p. 115.

...five men have perished by disease to one who has fallen by the sword. The articles most important for the preservation and health of the soldier in this wet and cold winter, I mean the article of shoes, in a miserable condition — to say nothing of the manner in which they are put together, the leather with which they are made, really does not deserve its name, but is a substance almost as porous as a sponge. The winter clothing instead of being forwarded in the month of October to protect the men from the terrible November of this climate rarely, or never comes to hand before the middle of winter, by which time the constitution of the recruit is broken and destroyed.

I pretend to no great experience, but since 1811 have been almost constantly with troops of some description or other, on the Canadian frontier, and I declare to you that the number of men killed in battle is but trifling when compared with that occasioned by the want of care which the health and comfort of the soldier requires.

Daily diet should have consisted of salt pork, hard bread, molasses, vinegar, salt and a daily ration of rum, whisky or brandy, and a few vegetables. But most of the time, at least a few of these items were not available. Sometimes there were none at all. Local farmers and their wives were allowed to sell vegetables, butter, pies and cooked meat to the soldiers, but their prices were greatly inflated.

Sanitation was primitive and caused illness. General Winfield Scott, as part of his training regime, required soldiers to bathe three times a week in a lake rather than a creek so they would not be contaminating drinking water. Often, waste pits were open and too near soldiers' living and eating areas.

Cholera, dysentery, typhus, hernia, hemorrhoids, and "fevers," a broad name for any undetermined disease, ague and food poisoning. Treatment was often the giving of emetics to induce vomiting, and blood-letting which was sometimes done by the use of leeches. The only drugs were opium, alcohol, quinine for malaria. Calomel, acetite of lead, and tartrite of ammonia were all used in treating dysentery, but they could, and probably did, cause death if taken in large doses.

An Officer's View

The building of Fort Henry started in 1812. Situated on a high promontory just outside Kingston, Ontario, it protected the Royal Naval Dockyard and base for the British navy on Lake Ontario. It was the second most strategic point (after Montreal) because of its location on Lake Ontario at the beginning of the one-thousand mile long St. Lawrence River.

Jacques Viger, was a captain in the Voltigeurs Canadiens, which was the Provincial Corps of Light Infantry, part of the force that built the fort at Port Henry. He was an officer with a valet, so his living conditions were much better than that of an ordinary soldier. They not only had to face the usual hardships of campaigns, but scarcity of food and supplies.

Source: Jacques Viger, *Reminiscences of the War of 1812-1814, Being Portions of the Diary of a Captain of the "Voltigeurs Canadiens" While in Garrison at Kingston, etc.*, News Printing Company, 1895, pp. 14-17.

....we were ordered by General Prevost on the 17th of May to cross over to Point Henry, where we now occupy tents which we again once more put in a wilderness of stumps, fallen trees, boulders,

In the Barracks of the Canadian Voltigeurs
(Canadian Park Service)

and rocks of all sizes and shapes; sharing our blanket with reptiles of varied species; carrying out the precepts of the most self-sacrificing charity towards ten million insects and crawling abominations, the ones more voracious and disgusting than the others. Phlebotomized by the muskitoes, cut and dissected by gnats, blistered by the sand flies, on the point of being eaten alive by the hungry wood rats as soon as they shall have disposed of our provisions. Pray for us! Pray for us! ye pious souls.

Broken down with fatigue, drenched with rain, I enter my tent to find that the birds of the air have besmirched me with lime; I have no sooner sat on my only camp stool when a horrid toad springs on to my lap in a most familiar way; I cast my wearied limbs on to my couch, a slimy snake insists on sharing with me the folds of my blanket, I hastily retire and leave him in possession. Let us have supper! The frying pan is produced to fry the ration pork. Horror! A monstrous spider has selected it for his web; he holds the fort in a viciously threatening attitude in the centre of its rays, he defiantly seems to say, remove me if you dare! The flinty biscuit must be pounded and broken or one can't eat it, here again the beastly wood-bug must needs crawl under the masher, and in losing his life infect everything with his sickening odor. Oh! Captain, what can we do? exclaims my valet. Fiat lux! Light the candle, you blockhead, light the candle. Let us write to our distant friends the excess of our misery. O ye gods, what a place this is! The candle is lighted, it is the next moment surrounded by myriads of flying things. My table is littered with writhing abominations, June bugs hasten from all sides, they besiege the light, extinguish it under one's very nose, strike you in the eye, and as a parting shot stun you with a blow on the forehead. What a paradise this spot would be for an entomologist!...

The Burning of Washington

By 1813, British ships were sailing up and down the Atlantic coast. In August 1814, the army stormed ashore and headed for Washington.

On August 23 the British landed near the young nation's capital. Within twenty-four hours, the White House and other public buildings were torched.

This view of the burning of Washington appeared in 1815 in the Stationer's Almanack in London. (Library of Congress)

The British then advanced on nearby Baltimore, where they met incredible resistance at Fort McHenry.

Fort McHenry, under attack of the British fleet. (Maryland Historical Society)

The Treaty of Ghent

The treaty to end the war became a reality on December 24, 1814. The document made no reference to the early conflicts over naval rights, neutrality, impressment, or territorial changes. In fact, almost all aspects of the treaty returned both nations to their pre-war status. The military strength of Britain had kept Canada from the grasp of expansionist Americans.

Although Indian uprisings in Florida had been stirred up during the war, Andrew Jackson had made a stir of his own, in a brutal slaughter of the Creeks in Alabama.

During the peace negotiations in Ghent, Belgium, American representatives — John Quincy Adams, Albert Gallatin, and Henry Clay — demanded land in Canada and Florida, but were unwilling to agree with the British on creating a neutral buffer state between American and British lands, so no borders changed. Indeed, it seemed that the entire war had been unnecessary!

Andrew Jackson

The War was over, but the fighting was not...

As British forces approached New Orleans in the last days of the War of 1812, Andrew Jackson issued this appeal for help on September 21, 1814.

Source: *Niles Weekly Register 7*, (December 1814): 205, found in William Loren Katz, *Eyewitness: A Living Documentary of the African American Contribution to American History*, New York: Simon and Schuster, 1995. pp. 70-71.

Andrew Jackson Appeals to Black New Orleans
PROCLAMATION
To the free colored inhabitants of Louisiana.

Through a mistaken policy you have heretofore been deprived of a participation in the glorious struggle for national rights in which our country is engaged. This no longer shall exist.

As sons of freedom, you are now called upon to defend our most inestimable blessing. As Americans, your country looks with confidence to her adopted children, for a valorous support, as a faithful return for the advantages enjoyed under her mild and equitable government. As fathers, husbands, and brothers, you are summoned to rally round the standard of the Eagle, to defend all which is dear in existence.

Your country, although calling for your exertions, does not wish you to engage in her cause, without amply remunerating you for the services rendered. Your intelligent minds are not to be led away by false representations. —Your love of honor would cause you to despise the man who should attempt to deceive you. In the sincerity of a soldier, and the language of truth I address you.

To every noble hearted, generous, freeman of color, volunteering to serve during the present contest with Great Britain, and no longer, there will be paid the same bounty, in money and lands, now received by the white soldiers of the U. States, viz. one hundred and twenty-four dollars in money, and one hundred and sixty acres of land. The non-commissioned officers and privates will also be entitled to the same monthly pay and daily rations, and clothes furnished to any American soldier.

On enrolling yourselves in companies, the major-general commanding will select officers for your government, from your white fellow citizens. Your non-commissioned officers will be appointed from among yourselves.

Due regard will be paid to the feelings of freemen and soldiers. You will not, by being associated with white men in the same corps, be exposed to improper comparisons or unjust sarcasm. As a distinct, independent battalion or regiment, pursuing the path of glory, you will, undivided, receive the applause and gratitude of your countrymen.

To assure you of the sincerity of my intentions and my anxiety to engage your invaluable services to our country, I have communicated my wishes to the governor of Louisiana, — who is fully informed as to the manner of enrollment, and will give you every necessary information on the subject of this address.

Headquarters, 7th military district,
Mobile, Sept. 21st 1814
Andrew Jackson,
Maj-gen, commanding

As the British prepared for their final attack on New Orleans, General Jackson reviewed the six thousand troops under his command. Of this force, about five hundred were African Americans in two battalions.

The Battle of New Orleans

The greatest American victory of the war came in a battle waged fifteen days after the Treaty of Ghent had been signed. In an attempt to solidify their right to navigate the Mississippi River, the British attacked New Orleans on January 8, 1815. Word had not yet arrived from Europe of the official end of the war, and in this final conflict, Andrew Jackson and his rag-tag forces of pirates, Creoles, freed slaves, and a group of Kentuckians were ready. The British lost 700 soldiers and had another 10,000 taken as prisoner or wounded. The Americans had only 13 dead and 58 wounded. The overwhelming victory of Jackson's lifted the spirits of Americans and brought new unity to America's political institutions.

On January 8th, a large British force was defeated by Andrew Jackson. (Courtesy of the Henry Francis DuPont Winterthur Museum.)

Consequences of the War

by
Mary Alice Burke Robinson

The War of 1812 is often seen as little more than a series of mistakes, fought by bumbling officers leading poorly-trained, ill-equipped men. Some say that it should not have been fought at all, that nothing that caused the war was even mentioned in the peace treaty. Does that mean that the War of 1812 was pointless? Was nothing decided?

Although the Treaty of Ghent officially ended the war, Canadians remained uneasy about their more aggressive neighbors to the south. They fortified Halifax, Kingston, and Quebec, and built the Rideau Canal, a 126-mile long project linking Montreal and Lake Ontario via Ottawa and Kingston. The canal, with 47 locks and 24 dams, provided a safe route in case the United States cut off the upper St. Lawrence River. Still a working canal, it is popular with pleasure boaters.

Canada restricted American immigration. British regiments disbanded in Canada and were given land there. Nearly 2,000 blacks settled in Nova Scotia and New Brunswick (many were slaves who had escaped on British ships during raids on the American coast). British were encouraged to emigrate to Upper Canada, Nova Scotia, and New Brunswick. Between 1815 and 1841, 600,000 people left Britain for Canada.

On the surface, the war seemed to be about freedom to trade freely without the control of another country, and the abolition of the impressment of American seamen. But a more significant issue was actually being resolved — the opening of the west for white settlers.

After the War of 1812 there would be no stopping the flow of pioneers West. And, to make the West more or less safe for settlers, the government sanctioned the defeat, dispersal, and near annihilation of the Native American tribes.

Although in later years a few attempts were made by Indians to stop westward expansion, it was too late. The defeat at The Prophet's Village at Tippecanoe Creek by William Henry Harrison, and the defeat of the Creek nation at the Tallushatchee towns by Andrew Jackson, were decisive. Like so many other ironies of this war, they are not usually considered actual battles of the War of 1812. But they were, and they sealed the fate of the Native American Indians.

Some say that the War of 1812 was a draw. But, it is easy to tell who really lost the war: the Native Americans. Tecumseh's dream of an independent Indian state, supported by Great Britain, died with him. No one else at that time had his ability to unite the tribes; no one had his vision. Tecumseh was the one man who might have been able to make his Indian brothers see the value and necessity of presenting a united front. But there was no one of his stature to carry on his work. When Britain signed the Treaty of Ghent, and withdrew to Canada, the Native Americans lost their last hope of containing the white man. The westward expansion movement was inevitable and could not, from that time on, be stopped.

In 1816, Albert Gallatin, who had been one of the negotiators who drew up the Treaty at Ghent, spoke of one major result of the War of 1812.

Source: Captain A. T. Mahan, *Sea Power In Its Relation to the War of 1812*, London, 1902, Vol. II, p. 436.

The war has renewed and reinstated the national feelings and character which the Revolution had given, and which were daily lessening. The people now have more general objects of attachment, with which their pride and political opinions are connected. They are more Americans; they feel and act more as a nation, and I hope that the permanency of the Union is thereby better secured.

Sadly, the Union was not secure. It is ironic that in about fifty years, the secessionist movement should come from the South on the issue of State's Rights, when the Hartford Convention might have brought an end to the United States in 1814. Delegates from most of the New England states met secretly in Hartford, Connecticut to discuss their opposition to federal government policy, even considering withdrawal from the union. The Treaty of Ghent brought an end to this movement and the Convention was dissolved in early 1815. But the issue of States' rights festered until settled by the Civil War, not quite fifty years later.

In July, 1963, the Ontario-St. Lawrence Development commission placed a plaque at Crysler's Farm, near Morrisburg, Ontario, in commemoration of the 150th anniversary of the battle there. Its beautiful message succinctly catches the spirit of the relationship between these two countries.

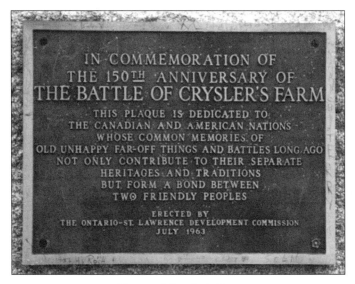

IN COMMEMORATION OF
THE 150TH ANNIVERSARY OF
THE BATTLE OF CRYSLER'S FARM
THIS PLAQUE IS DEDICATED TO
THE CANADIAN AND AMERICAN NATIONS
WHOSE COMMON MEMORIES OF
OLD UNHAPPY FAR-OFF THINGS AND BATTLES LONG AGO
NOT ONLY CONTRIBUTE TO THEIR SEPARATE
HERITAGES AND TRADITIONS
BUT FORM A BOND BETWEEN
TWO FRIENDLY PEOPLES
ERECTED BY
THE ONTARIO-ST. LAWRENCE DEVELOPMENT COMMISSION
JULY 1963

Plaque at Crysler's Farm
(Photo by Mary Alice Burke Robinson)

Today the 3,000 mile United States-Canadian border is the longest undefended border in the world.

Suggested Further Reading

Note: Books cited throughout the text are also recommended.

Brown, Duncan. *The Monkey's Constitution*. Carlisle, MA: Discovery Enterprises, Ltd., 1997. (Juvenile/YA historical fiction about a "powder monkey" on the USS *Constitution* in her battle against the *Guerriere* in the War of 1812.)

Ferris, Jean. *Into the Wind*. New York, Avon, 1996.

Fritz, Jean. *The Great Little Madison*. New York, G. P. Putnam's Sons, 1989. (Juvenile historical fiction)

Gay, Kathlyn and Gay. *War of 1812*. New York, Holt, 1995.

Gerson, Noel B. *The Velvet Glove*. New York, Thomas Nelson Inc., 1975.

Henderson, James. *Sloops and Brigs*. Naval Institute Press, 1972.

Ibbitson, John. *1812: A Novel*. Maxwell Macmillan Canada, 1991.

Litt, Paul, Ronald F. Williamson, and Joseph W. A. Whitehorne. *Death at Snake Hill: Secrets From a War of 1812 Cemetery*. Toronto, Dundurn Press, 1993.

Lord, Walter. *The Dawn's Early Light*. New York, W. W. Norton and Company, Inc. 1972.

McKenzie, Ruth. *Laura Secord: The Legend and the Lady*. Toronto, McClelland and Steward Ltd., 1971.

Morris, Richard B. *The War of 1812*. Minneapolis, Lerner Publications, 1985.

Nevin, David. *1812*. New York, Tom Doherty Association, 1996.

Turner, Wesley. *The War of 1812: The War That Both Sides Won*. Toronto, Dundurn Press, 1990.